Critters of Creation

Tell of God's Love

Lisa Maheu

WestBow Press books may be ordered through booksellers or by contacting:

WestBow Press
A Division of Thomas Nelson & Zondervan
1663 Liberty Drive
Bloomington, IN 47403
www.westbowpress.com
844-714-3454

Interior Image Credit: Lala Maheu

ISBN: 979-8-3850-0370-9 (sc)
ISBN: 979-8-3850-0371-6 (e)

Library of Congress Control Number: 2023913797

Print information available on the last page.

WestBow Press rev. date: 08/17/2023

WESTBOW
PRESS
A DIVISION OF THOMAS NELSON
& ZONDERVAN

To Parents from the Author,

Time spent with your child is a precious commodity. Reading to and with your child helps them learn phonics. Phonological awareness is the ability to play with sounds in language. There are different levels of skills in phonological awareness. Rhyming is one. A rhyme is a recurrence of similar sounds at the end of words. The repetition of words, ideas and skills is important for early brain development.

As you are reading to your child, you are also teaching them the importance of the concepts of print and how reading itself works. Some of the ways you can teach your child the importance of print is by showing them books have:

- A cover and a back
- A title
- An author and illustrator
- Pages that are read from top to bottom and left to right.
- Sentences that begin with capital letters and end with punctuation (a period, question mark or exclamation mark).

You will notice the words, **"God loves me,"** printed in bold text at the beginning of each stanza. As you read, say these words loudly, this helps your child to remember the concept that God loves them in all the things they do.

There are also scriptures at the end of each page that are related to each thought. It is important for children to memorize scripture because it helps them learn to be more like Jesus in every way.

In the back of the book are interesting facts about each animal along with questions to help encourage children to use critical thinking, and to support a better understanding about their relationship with God.

I pray as you read this book to your child, you both create a love for reading and most importantly a love for God our Father.

Lisa Maheu

Does God love me I ask myself every day?

"Yes", He answers, "let me show you the way."

"And so we know the love that God has for us, and we trust that love. God is love." 1 John 4:16

God loves me as the story is told.

This is news for everyone young and old.

"So know that the Lord your God is God. He is the faithful God. He will keep his agreement of love for a thousand lifetimes. He does this for people who love him and obey his commands." Deuteronomy 7:9

God loves me that He gave me eyes that I may see.

So, I can gaze upon a lovely butterfly high above a tree.

"Open my eyes to see the wonderful things in your teachings." Psalm 119:18

God loves me when I use my ears I heard,

The sound of a tweet or cry from a bird.

"The Lord has made both these things: Ears that can hear and eyes that can see." Proverbs 20:12

God loves me when I am happy, I can feel.

The soft touch of a tickle that makes me squeal.

"But the Spirit gives love, joy, peace, patience, kindness, goodness, faithfulness, gentleness, self-control."
Galatians 5:22

God loves me as high as the stars.

But God is always near not far.

"Give thanks to the God of heaven. His love continues forever." Psalms 136:26

God loves me as I walk through the tall grass that grows.

Cause I can feel a caterpillar on my ten toes.

"And on your feet wear the Good News of peace to help you stand strong."
Ephesians 6:15

God loves me like no other.

Better than my father or mother.

"Dear friends, we should love each other, because love comes from God."
1 John 4:7

God loves me while I sleep.

A promise He will always keep.

"You won't need to be afraid when you lie down. When you lie down, your sleep will be peaceful." Proverbs 3:24

God loves me when I am feeling sorrow.

His love endures then, now, and even tomorrow.

"He will wipe away every tear from their eyes. There will be no more death, sadness, crying or pain." Revelation 21:4

God loves me morning, noon, and night.

He takes away my fear and fright.

"Where God's love is there is no fear, because God's perfect love takes away fear." 1 John 4:18

God loves me when I feel happy.

Like a hug that feels soft and cuddly.

"Be full of joy in the Lord always. I will say again, be full of joy." Philippians 4:4

God loves me while I run and play.

His love lasts throughout the day.

"And the streets will be filled with boys and girls playing." Zechariah 8:5

God loves me when I sit down to eat.

He helps me taste sour, bitter, salty, or sweet.

"So, if you eat, or if you drink, or if you do anything, do everything for the glory of God." *1 Corinthians 10:31*

God loves me when I feel ill.

He helps me take that nasty pill.

"The Lord will give him strength when He is sick. The Lord will make him well again." Psalms 41:3

God loves me even when I am bad.

Because He is my loving Dad.

"I will be your father, and you will be my sons and daughters, says the Lord All-Powerful."

2 Corinthians 6:18

God loves me when I feel grumpy.

He makes me laugh at something funny.

"Always be happy." 1 Thessalonians 5:16

God loves me when I feel lonely.

He longs to be my friend and buddy.

"I love you people with a love that will last forever. I became your friend because of my love and kindness." Jeremiah 31:3

God loves me in the same way as a loving mother.

He protects me like a bird by hovering over.

"The Lord of heaven's armies will defend Jerusalem. He will defend it like birds flying over their nests." Isaiah 31:5

God loves me when I talk to Him and pray.

He hears and answers in a loving, caring way.

"Never stop praying." 1 Thessalonians 5:17

God loves me this I know.

Because Jesus Christ told me so.

"For God loved the world so much that He gave His only Son. God gave His Son so that whoever believes in Him may not be lost but have eternal life." John 3:16

Interesting facts and questions.

Chickens- A long time ago, chickens once roamed the land as wild birds. They were simple to catch and easy to take care of, so people started raising them on farms. Chickens have been around for a long time. Before people had alarm clocks, they used roosters to help them wake up to start a new day. God has been around for a long time. He loved His people then and He still loves us today. He will never stop loving us.

Questions to ask:
- What is the red skin on top of a chicken's head called? *(a comb or crest)*
- How do we know God has been around since the beginning of time? *(The Bible tells us so in the book of Genesis 1:1)*

Blue morpho butterfly- The blue morpho butterfly is a beautiful insect found in the Amazon Forest. Blue is an extremely rare color in nature. These butterflies have scales that overlap, refracting light like a prism. So, when the light hits the butterfly's wings, it is bent against the scales and comes off as blue. God created so many colors in nature for us to enjoy.

Questions to ask:
- What are some animals that God created?
- What are some of God's creations that are blue? *(Ocean, sky, one color of the rainbow, blue whale, a person's blue eyes)*.

California quails- A quail's call is usually used as a way of communicating to gather the other quails. The sound is usually made when a flock is about to move from one place to another. This sound is also made when a bird has gotten separated from the others. It makes the sound repeatedly so the others can hear the cry and reply to him. The noise made by a male quail sounds like they are singing, "Wet my lips." God has given us the beautiful gift of hearing, that we may hear our loved ones. It is one of the five senses.

Questions to ask:
- Where do quails like to live? *(Fields and meadows)*
- Think of five different animals. What sounds do they make?

Zebras- A zebra sounds more like a donkey but sometimes their sounds are like barks or snorts. Do zebras laugh? Zebras laugh to express excitement and contentment. Laughing helps us feel better, removing sorrow, relieve pain and stress. God wants us to laugh, to enjoy what He has given us. So, go ahead and laugh.

Questions to ask:
- What do you believe? Are zebras white with black stripes or black with white stripes? *(Zebras have black skin, so zebras are black with white stripes)*
- What joke or funny story can you tell someone to make them laugh?

Birds- Did you know birds can hover as high as airplanes without facing any sort of trouble? Some birds can reach an altitude of 40,000 feet. It may seem that God is far away, but He is closer than you think.

Questions to ask:
- Can you remember a time when you felt alone? How did it make you feel?
- Why does praying to God make you feel better?

Caterpillar- A caterpillar has one job, to eat. They must increase their body mass by as much as 1,000 times or more. A caterpillar has as many as 4,000 muscles in its body and has 16 legs. No wonder they tickle when they crawl on you. God has given us our five senses, one of those is the sense of touch.

Questions to ask:
- What are other ways you can use your sense of touch? *(Your skin has many different sense receptors. The most sensitive parts of your skin have the most receptors like your fingers, toes, and lips. Using your sense of touch helps you feel if something is hot or cold, wet, or dry, rough, or smooth.*

Brown bears- Bears are extraordinarily intelligent animals. They care deeply for their family members. Bears grieve deeply for others. Cubs are known to moan and cry when separated from their mothers. Just like our parents, mother bears are affectionate, protective, devoted, strict, sensitive, with their young. Even though we are loved by our parents, God loves us much more than that.

Questions to ask:
- What are baby bears called? *(cubs)*
- Can you name some ways God loves you?

Penguins- When temperatures drop down to -50°C with winds of up to 200km/hr., Emperor's penguins must adapt to the harsh weather to survive. They have two layers of feathers, a good reserve of fat, smaller beaks, and flippers to prevent heat loss. Emperors also have feathers on their legs, so their ankles don't get too chilly. Colonies of adults and chicks work together to huddle for warmth. Up to 5,000 adults and chicks shuffle around, taking turns from the outside of the huddle where it is cold. They stay like this even during the night to sleep, protecting each other, just like God watches over us while we sleep.

Pray for nighttime:

God our Father, thank you for my home, bed and loved ones. Help me to rest well and to give me peaceful dreams. Watch over me during the night. Teach me to love and trust you more each day. Amen.

Brown bunny- Rabbits are very social creatures that live in groups. Rabbits perform an athletic leap, known as a "binky" when they're happy, performing twists and kicks in midair! So, when you are feeling sad, pray to God for comfort.

You can recite a simple prayer like this when you feel sad.

God today my heart feels sad. Help me to remember funny things that make me laugh. Thank you even when I feel sad you are there to make me feel happy again. Amen.

Alligators- Since alligators are cold blooded, they are usually seen sunning on top of rocks. Sometimes, they lay out with their mouths held open, this is not a sign of aggression but instead is a natural tactic to help regulate body temperature to help them keep cool. So, to keep your cool when you are afraid, pray to God for peace.

Question to ask:
- Why is it important to pray to God when you are afraid?
- What is the difference between alligators and crocodiles? *(Alligators have a wider, U-shaped snout, while crocodiles have a pointier, V-shaped snout. While alligators love to live in fresh water, crocodiles like saltwater).*

Lion and tiger cubs- Lion and tiger cubs are very playful when they are not sleeping. You can see them often playing around with each other. They love to snuggle because they are very affectionate towards one another. The cubs also love to wrestle with their siblings, mother, or father. When playing, a cub can often be seen leaping on another's back and biting their neck. Playing with each other helps the cubs learn to hunt. When you're feeling happy, give someone a hug. It can make you and the other person feel special and loved. God loves it when we show love to others.

Questions to ask:
- Who teaches the lion cubs to hunt? *(Female lioness)*
- True or False? Lion cubs spend a lot of time playing or sleeping during their first few months. *(True)*
- How old is a tiger cub when it starts to hunt? *(Tiger cubs start learning to hunt around eight to ten months old. Training with their mother).*

Pigs- Pigs are playful, friendly, sensitive, and intelligent animals. They've long been considered smarter than dogs. Much like people, pigs are soothed by music, love playing ball, and even enjoy getting massages. During Bible times, children played with toys made from clay, wood, or stones. They also played sports games like racing, tug-of-war, or wrestling. God loves it when we play, it helps us feel good inside.

Can you think of fun ways to play?
You can pretend to:
- *Climb the highest mountain.*
- *Swim to the bottom of the ocean.*
- *Fly as high as the birds.*

- *Race with friends on your bike.*
- *See who can jump the farthest.*
- *Play your favorite game of ball.*

Orangutans- Orangutans eat fruits, leaves, bark, nuts, seeds, insects, and honey. They prefer the sweet fruit of bananas and melons, but they also need leaves and bark to stay healthy. God gave us the sense of taste to enjoy all kinds of healthy food.

Questions to ask:
- What are some healthy foods that God created?
- Why do we need healthy foods?

Beavers- Beavers love to eat barks and twigs from poplar, aspen, birch, willow, and maple trees. Sometimes, critters like the beaver can get infected with a variety of diseases. Scientists have studied animals in the wild and have observed that some plant species are used by animals to help them feel better. These plants may not taste good, but they help the critters become healthy. God has given us natural plants and herbs to help us when we are sick. He has also given doctors the wisdom to know how to make us better.

Questions to ask:
- Talk about a time when you were sick. How did you feel?
- Why do you have to take medicine or go to the doctor when you are ill?

Gorillas- The silverback male gorilla has a responsibility to its family, or clan, which may contain several dozen gorillas. He must find food for the whole group, as well as defend them from other predators. Male gorillas have been seen snuggling with the infants and playing with them. God our Heavenly Father may not always approve of our bad behavior, but like our parents He always loves us. His love endures forever.

Talk to your child about a time they did not obey. Use some of these questions to start a conversation.
- How do you feel when someone asks you to do something, and you say "no"?
- How do you feel when you lie to someone?
- Do you believe God loves you even when you are bad? Why?

Chameleon- When you watch a chameleon, you might wonder about their eyes. Chameleons can rotate their eyes at almost 342 degrees, and the eyes move independently from each other. Without moving their head, they can look at their surroundings to search for prey. They can even rotate each eye independently in different directions. Watching a chameleon rotate their eyes can seem quite funny. Go ahead and laugh, God wants us to be happy even when we feel grumpy. Sometimes children don't always know why they feel cranky. Memorizing scripture can help them overcome some anxieties.

Here are some memory verses they can remember during times of stress.
- *"Do not worry about anything. But pray and ask God for everything you need." Philippians 4:6*
- *"So don't worry because I am with you." Isaiah 41:10*
- *"Remember that I commanded you to be strong and brave. So don't be afraid. The Lord your God will be with you everywhere you go." Joshua 1:9*

Red Panda- Red panadas are very territorial and do live alone. They love to climb trees and can descend headfirst. Like giant pandas, red pandas are a bamboo-munching species native to high forests of Asia. These furry cute little critters are closely related to racoons than pandas.

Ask your child, have they ever felt alone. Explain to them that they are never alone with Jesus. Have them repeat this little prayer with you.
- *Jesus is my best friend. I can always talk to Him anytime. I can talk to Him any place. I am never alone when I talk to Jesus. Jesus, I love you and I feel loved when you are near. Amen.*

Eagle- Some of the characteristics of an eagle are strength, tenderness, a sharp sense of sight, a swift gift of flight and loyalty. During incubation, one parent stays on the nest for warmth and protection, while the other hunts for food and watches the nest from nearby. Eagles are often seen soaring high above hills and rocky cliffs. When eagles fly, they do not flap their wings like other birds. Instead, they spread their wings and glide across the sky. This allows the eagle to fly for a long time without getting tired. The parent eagles are very protective of their young. Even though God is high above in heaven, He hovers over us and protects us always. He is our loving Father and will never leave us.

Questions to ask:
- What are baby eagles called? *(eaglets)*
- What is another name for an eagle's sharp claws? *(talons)*

Barn owl- Owls are solitary animals, which means they like to be alone. When other birds come close to their nests, an owl will warn them to stay away with a "hoot-hoot" sound. The Barn Owl loves to make their nests in human-made structures such as buildings. In some parts of the world, an owl can be found using church steeples as nest sites. That's a nice way to be close to God. Another way to be close to God is when we pray. Praying has always been important to people who believe in God. Jesus prayed often to God. God is always ready to hear prayers. He hears and answers the prayers of everyone who has faith in Him.

Questions to ask:
- What is praying? *(Talking to God)*
- When can you talk to God? *(Anytime, anywhere)*

Dolphins- Why do dolphins jump out of the water? Dolphins jump in the wild for several reasons. When traveling, they use less energy jumping than swimming. Dolphins can move a long distance with one long jump. Dolphins also jump to find food. Dolphins are playful intelligent animals and sometimes they jump just for fun. We can leap for joy knowing that God loves us so much that He sent His son Jesus, to Earth to tell us about Him. Jesus is God's gift to us. We learn this by reading the Bible. The Bible is a special book that tells us about God. Jesus died on the cross, but He came back to life and proved He is the Son of God.

Questions to ask:
What is your favorite way to spend time with God and learn about Him? Draw a picture of you spending time with God.

All Scripture is from International Children's Bible

Printed in the United States
by Baker & Taylor Publisher Services